Arachnid Verve

FIRST EDITION, 2016

Arachnid Verve
© 2016 by Shauna Osborn

ISBN 978-0-9972517-1-5

Except for fair use in reviews and/or scholarly considerations, no part of this book may be reproduced, performed, recorded, or otherwise transmitted without the written consent of the author and the permission of the publisher.

Cover Art
"Scorpion & Spider" illustration by W.I. Bicknell from *The Natural History of the Sacred Scriptures, and Guide to General Zoology* (1851)

Author Photo
"Self Portrait" by Shauna Osborn

MONGREL EMPIRE PRESS
NORMAN, OK

ONLINE CATALOGUE: WWW.MONGRELEMPIRE.ORG

This publisher is a proud member of

COUNCIL OF LITERARY MAGAZINES & PRESSES
w w w . c l m p . o r g

Arachnid Verve

Shauna Osborn

2016

Acknowledgements

Grateful recognition goes to the editors & readers of the following publications in which these poems first appeared: *About Place, Adrienne, Agave Magazine, As/Us: A Space for Women of the World, Commonthought, Cultural Weekly, Cyclamens and Swords, East Jasmine Review, Hueso Loco, Literary Orphans, Mas Tequila Review, Poiesis, Prosaic, Red Ink, Skin to Skin, Spiral Orb, Toe Good, Upstreet, Veils, Halos, & Shackles: International Poetry on the Oppression and Empowerment of Women Anthology, Waxwing, Yellow Medicine Review,* and *Zouch Magazine.*

The fullest of gratitude belongs to all the co-conspirators, inspirations, family, & friends who helped shape this work over the past several years—y'all know who you are. Also, a big appreciation to the individuals that made this physical book manifest—from the ones making the paper & ink to those editing, printing, & working on design.

Muchas gracias mis amores.

Contents

~Antes Taabe (Before the Sun) — 1

Animalia/Arthropoda/Arachnida/Araneae
- Memoir — 5
- Boiled Beets In Late June — 6
- Double Standard — 8
- Toothpaste on Toast — 10
- Less Than Permanent — 11
- Domestic Defense — 12
- Dishwater — 13
- Spin Cycle — 15
- Split Tongued — 19

Indra's Net
- Truss — 23
- From Wind & Earth — 24
- Mangoes in Early Fall — 25
- Marked — 26
- One Clover, One Bee — 28
- Altitude — 29
- Indra's Net — 34
- Unbound — 35
- Snake Song — 36

Aso & Anansi
- Morning Bus — 41
- Tom Robbins And The Film-Covered Penis — 42
- Plan B — 44
- The Edge Of Senlis — 48
- Vignettes — 50
- Technosexual — 53
- Insight — 55
- Remnants — 57
- Thirty-Five — 58
- No Sad Songs In The House Of The Sun — 59
- Doppelgänger — 62

Filament, Filament, Filament
- Animus/Anima — 65
- Women Who'd Float Away — 67
- When Clouds Sizzle — 68
- Song for Nina — 69
- Xing — 71

Respite	72
The Judd Nelson Habit	75
Wing	76
On Guadalupe Bridge	79
Guionista Sangre (Blood Writer)	81
A Full Measure's Rest	85
Glossary of Potentially Unfamiliar Terms	89

~Antes Taabe (Before the Sun)

this is how all our stories begin:

from fingers
from feathers black & red
ink drips across the page

write
write of water
write of puehpi y tucan—
scales & feathers
write of painted sands
& sea foam
in the season of taabe
write

& with each new corrido
a storm of bloodied feathers
whip across your face
cerca de tu cuerpo
& land soundless
at your feet

Animalia / Arthropoda / Arachnida / Araneæ

My mother says when I get older my dusty hair will settle and my blouse will learn to stay clean, but I have decided not to grow up tame . . .

—Sandra Cisneros
House on Mango Street

Memoir

Tell me your story—Marύawe
Mine begins inside a rubbish can of tarnished steel
Where cirrus clouds surrounded by azure stirred between
        an arching border of gray

& my stubby toddler legs were stuck straight up as if to use
        the rim as a quay
To launch myself promptly onto an invisible craft with vertical keel
Tell me your story— Marύawe

Surrounded by siblings as bright & boisterous as only
        Oklahoma jays
Could breed, cackling as if they alone knew the treasures some
        trashcans conceal
Where cirrus clouds surrounded by azure stirred between an
        arching border of gray

Upon a bed of crumpled newsprint and pungent diner scraps
        I did lay
Until mother felt my absence & retrieved me with a rush of
        anxiety & zeal
Tell me your story— Marύawe

Mine begins alone, at peace, & tranquil before my mother's fray
Discovering a domicile amongst someone else's refuse &
        the abject surreal
Where cirrus clouds surrounded by azure stirred between an
        arching border of gray

Rhythmically tapping my foot on the metal wall as I stared at that
        which I could survey
I gained consciousness amongst wrappers with leftover ketchup &
        gravy to congeal
Tell me your story— Marύawe
Where cirrus clouds surrounded by azure stirred between an
        arching border of gray

Boiled Beets In Late June

The pungent smell of hot compote comes wafting
out all the open windows & doors of grandma's house.

The smell grows stronger near the kitchen stove, where large
red stained stew pots are bubbling with this year's beet crop.

Humid Oklahoma heat is incredible even without burners going
& the smell makes the inside of the house impossible to bear.

We sit out on the front porch, far away from windows,
                snapping peas
& hoping to stir some breeze with accordion folded paper fans.

Sweat stings my eyes as I brush flies away from my mouth
& the large metal bowl gathering shucked black eye peas.

I want to swim in a bathtub of ice chips. Move my chair to a
walk in freezer. Smother myself in Otter pops.

No one wants to hear me complain.
Mother, Aunt Ann, & Grandma all work these fields.

Brutal summer heat is just as expected to them as having dirty
                laundry at the end of each day.
I count the times Ann laughs after Grandma mumbles
"Goddamned mosquitoes" & swats at her arm.

Fifty-six before the pots of boiled bastards are done &
we can leave the sun.

We turn all the electric fans full blast. I tie a bandana
around my nose & mouth to block the smell of beet blood.

We sit at the kitchen table; pour ladles of hot beet into
clean Mason jars. My nose grows numb.

The walls will smell for weeks
even after a long scrub.

Bleach can't take away thirty years of grease
caked on the once neutral walls.

Nicotine yellow becomes the answer
sanity, along with cash, saved.

Grandmother repainted her walls only once.
White went tarnished in hours.

Grit filled crevices showed first, then spread.
Smoke staying in both the paint & lungs.

So we covered windows, table, & couch
with eggshell colored plastic doilies & moved on.

Grandma swears that shade doesn't matter much.
A wall is a wall, grime yellow or pale vivid white.

Mother prefers wallpaper.

Double Standard

I.
"If you were a man,"
he said as he threw
my t-shirt roughly towards
my short pudgy body,
never taking his eyes
off the plank board
& table saw in front of him,
"it wouldn't be wrong."
"But Daddy..."
"No buts!
That's the way it is.
Now put your damn
shirt back on
before someone
sees you & go help
your grandmother
in the kitchen
if it's so goddamn
hot outside."

Eight year old
fists throw hammer
& nails onto
concrete deck
& tug the gray
Ghostbusters shirt
slowly over sweaty shoulders
& offensive skin
feet kicking every bit
stone & stick
from garage to screen door.

Banished from the smell
of sawdust & dirt,
to the one of flour & grease—
from sun burnt backs
to crisp aprons,
periwinkle curtains
& cast iron skillets.

II.
"GODDAMN IT, CAUSE
THAT'S THE WAY IT IS,"
she says slamming down
the large yellow enamel bowl
full of tortilla dough onto
the worn wooden counter
powdered with loose flour & salt.
"If you were a man, I wouldn't worry.
But you're not. You're my girl and
shouldn't be stayin' all alone in that
big ass city."

Eighteen year old fist
tightens its grip on the
black handled steak knife
that chops potatoes into furious
thick brown skinned cubes &
sends shreds to cover the gray
Bulldog Basketball shirt
covering sweaty arms & shoulders
just back from practice.

"No more talkin' bout it.
Finish those 'taters & then
go outside to help your pa
feed them animals before it
gets dark."

Toothpaste on Toast

Todas las noches
para una semana
I spend the dark hours
before dawn
en el trailer amarillo
six years old
door closed
para el baño
sitting on the fake tile floor
between the toilet & sink
knees against my chest
or legs sprawled straight out
comer pasta de dientes en una tostada
until I wake up
the strange familiar
taste still in my mouth
veinticinco
y en mi cama
en nuestro apartamento
reminded
nuestra madre
sat door opened
between the tub & toilet
alta de la meth
chewing her fingernails
& begging me
hacernos tostadas
shut the door rápido
but come in & sit
down, no no aquí
pero aquí & sing

Less Than Permanent

You balance on bent knees
eyes focused on the paint
rolling slow from the saturated
bristles of our rusted brush
to your sun burnt arm
while I fix the stack
of cement bricks
that serve as our
front porch stairs

You tell me there's
nothing for us here
but the wind
& we will never be anything
to this town if we continue
to trade rosaries for
each plastic nametag
wear it
throw it next to the shoes

something else to move
something else to lose
under blue wrinkled bedspreads
& amongst empty cans
of beer & kidney beans:

One more thing
less than permanent

Domestic Defense

Conversations
of how to defend
front porches
with strategic
grenade patterns
continue after
the frizzy haired
gypsy, limp
hand-rolled
cigarette hanging
from her blue lips,
fails to convince
that the medicinal
herbs she has piled
on a wicker platter will
ever cure what ails me.

Real life is lived
in the chemically recycled
details; toasted carcinogens,
meat flavored nitrates, artificial cherry
cough syrups full of red dye #4, handfuls
of over-the-counter muscle relaxers, &
plastic Batman cups full of liquor
& carbonated high fructose corn syrup.
Even those defective childproof caps
serve the important purpose of making
one feel better.

Life, my herbal bag
holding friends, should be lived
like an unpinned grenade
near the porch swing.
We exist as a squib—
one sizzle,
a flash of teeth,
then you're out.

Dishwater

Some people could look at a mud puddle and see an ocean with ships.
—Zora Neale Hurston

cups

mugs &

coffee spoons

placid plastic

translucent glass

& stoneware

inhabited by

nymphs with

mid level concerns

like waste management

& cozy kitchen crannies

furry nymphs a hundred

shades of brown &

green dancing in

short delicate spirals

wishing the charm

would wear off

the golden finish chip

or tarnish & the

metal liquefy

into a thousand tiny ships sailing

due east watching

naval fleets pierced

by hardened shredded cheddar

& green grape seeds

the captain lost in a stare

thinking what the hell's the difference

between a cup & mug anyway

calling for the deck hands'

wanting to forget his post

to lose himself inside a large

citrus scented soap bubble

to be surrounded by

ethereal oscillating

pastels of

yellow

pink

& blue

Spin Cycle

Oh, you told me once, dear, that you loved me
You said that we never would part
But a link in the chain has been broken
Leaves me with a sad and aching heart

Outdoors: 1937
Lye soap bubbles over an open flame

Clothes spin around the cast iron pot
stirred with a thick wooden stick

My great grandma Ruthie's tiny frame
stoops slightly as she spits Skoal
into an empty Kerr jar, her stomach large
with its eighth child.

Using the end of her bough, she pulls
the clothes out one by one, each steaming
in the April morning air. She stretches the
dripping fabric over the low hanging branches
of the large oak tree upwind & yells to the
girls to start making beans for dinner.

Grandma's little babies love
shortnin' shortnin'
Grandma's little babies
love shortnin' bread

Indoors: 1986
A pot of beans boils on yellow ochre stove

My sister & I pull clothes
from the warm center
of the drying machine to a
white plastic hamper,
trying not to drag them
on the dust covered wood floor.

Grandma Lois picks up the flood of clothes
balancing it between thick hip & arm
tall above our heads with a
thin cigarette that dangles
between her lips. We dance our way
through the kitchen to fold in front
of the air conditioner & listen to Hank Williams.

Been a longtime gone
No I ain't hoed a row since I don't know when
Longtime gone
And it ain't comin' back again

Outdoors: 2000
White Ford truck driving down Jenkins Ave
with two passengers & plastic mugs of fresh coffee

Dead leaves fall on the windshield
while the stoplight stays red.

You rest your dark arms
on the steering wheel,
head bent as if you lost something
on the floorboards & ask
if there's a Laundromat
near my place, just in case.
You may need to stay
for a couple of days & borrow
some clothes until you find money.
I grimace & take a drink, then
answer a slow yes. From that moment,
quarters & fresh linen became sacred.

Awakened to cheers after years on the fault line
We are shocked to be here
In the face of the meantime
Pharaoh, all your methods have taught me
Is to separate my blood from bone

Indoors: 2004

Two lit cigarettes amongst the rows of yellow ochre
washers & avocado green plastic chairs

A $3 spin cycle continuum of
clanking buttons & cell phoned patrons
in rhythmic succession
during the stale static of bodily stasis
where I sit & wish for the rinse to be brief

You tell me of a little pouch
you once owned
to place your unmentionables in
while at the laundry.

Not for me, I say,
the type that'd swing
size six bikini briefs
above my head
for anyone to see.

You smile & nod.
Yes my lil' Amazon savage
    (fold fold stuff
    fold fold stuff)
There's nothing we can do
to clean you up.

Split Tongued

aikurekwatɨ
& you want to drown:

pensamientos completos
incomplete English

limping from your sluggish tongue

you walk until
Kwana kuhtsu paa

& drown yourself in small currents

nɨɨhtsi?aitɨ eeko pai
split tongued water

dividida lengua

drown in the muck
& scummy bubbles

u?hoikị mɨhɨ naape

flood the throat that refuses to sculpt
sounds pronounced smooth & soft

smash your tongue into the riverbed
that rises between your toes

& when water laps
encima tus oídos
hear the sound of voices
speaking their own language
in the rich wet sounds of earth

Indra's Net

Think of me as Shiva, a many-armed and -legged body with one foot on brown soil, one on white, one in straight society, one in the gay world, the man's world, the women's, one limb in the literary world, another in the working class, the socialist, and the occult worlds. A sort of spider woman hanging by one thin strand of web.

—Gloria Anzaldúa "La Prieta"

Truss

She wards the doorjamb.
I, the knob. Stuck in a
sitzkrieg, rotten with
dust & peppermint oil.

The spider clings to its mark,
persistent & intractable,
this black baby
that rebuilds its web
each time the north wind wails
or I open the screen door.

The bitsy arachnid refusing
to concede & allow any force to
relocate her home, no matter
how many times it tries.

The wind, the door,
the spider, & I now locked
into the perpetual dance
of obstinacies, destruction,
& repair.

From Wind & Earth

Bonded from different star bodies
forged from the sun
birthing people of
wind & earth
water & thread
fiery & vital
both singular & cacophonous
creating upright pliable vessels
of multiple conscious,
historic, & whole
spinning each day
a creation story

We began as dust
wind blown & reckless
whirling together
from each direction
losing our succinct
& elemental character
to blend atomically &
mold bodies of somewhat
solid flesh, chemically bonded
for blood, pus, spit & sweat
for skin, bone, cartilage, & fat

Mangoes in Early Fall

There's no civilized way to eat some fruits—
just savage sucking & ripping of flesh,
the large white seed in the center
waiting to be exposed. Bite into it
like an apple or a peach—such sweetness
drips down the throat, blonde fibers
much like corn silk & just as uneatable.
This exotic tropical fruit—only seen in
romantic comedies located in some
exotic place—never grown amongst
the pear trees & grape vines. & when
the large white seed with remaining amber
mohair is put on the plate with the
toughened shaved skin (read rind)
that couldn't be chewed, the poem is done
gone, left in the space of time that can only
be broken with teeth marks through inviting
red/green flesh

Marked

you remember hatching from a purple oval shell
[everyday a re-enactment
of the creation story] the feel
of someone rubbing the blades of your shoulders
that unfold ochre & maroon tinted wings
sticky with amniotic fluid

black charcoal haze cover m~~u~~a
cloud her face
& when you try to write
   to sketch
   to draw
she stands behind you
silent
distraught
eyes bandaged & bulging
in her hands she holds
a bouquet of bloodied brown feathers
which she drops one by one
to float zig zag across your line of vision
& pile upon the blank white page
the gray & silver stars
try to push through the holes &
in time your eyes are open
the sea foam green ceiling cracks & caves
all you hear is the wind
pushing through the window panes & busted rafters
the yutaibo medea begins to wail & thrash
as your hands become covered in black dust
opaque black dust that hovers
regardless of soap/bleach/steel wool
your skin becomes brittle & raw
& in your head you begin to scream
& in your head you are screaming blood
but from your larynx
a single simple sputter escapes

you feel cold marble under your slashed palms
you smell musk & branding irons from the
east as gloved hands clasp over your lips
your wings & arms cut
before artificial light scatters its luster
& every time you arch
your scaled back
or twist too far
either direction
you wince, you feel the
rough itch in your scars
as if your decayed wings
wish to sprout open anew,
feel the wind envelope
the taunt membrane
between your bones
& fly

One Clover, One Bee
for E.D.

We hardly know the Amherstian Bee
though many think that they love her
honey anointed lips

A queen bee buzzing
amongst apiaries, scouting
fields for pollen-heavy clovers
that haven't fattened a calf

One bee, one clover
over & over

Celestial ivory clad noble,
locked in her internal realm,
wishing stingers could sprout anew

Her revery, her eloquence
birthing prairies from
dormant badlands
& budding cityscapes

One clover, one bee
over & over

Altitude

I.
Sierras never lose their awe to a prairie field worker
too familiar with flat red earth used for harvest & dust

Whose voyage through fissures, switchbacks, and gorges
had only occurred on television or projection screens

As the ice covered giant shakes sheets of snow
onto the dirty interstate spiraling down its height

I thrust that treacherous metal forward
unable to turn the engine off

Hundreds of miles more before sleep
no matter how wretched roads go

With each slide, each loss of vision
due to dense snow, a grind of sore teeth

Each time outcrops come too close
or the rails become shrouded from headlights,

I recognize my stubbornness
will be the end of me

II.
A bathroom tile battle
between a broad hairy scorpion
and large black widow
awakes the once dormant
competitive fire from my ancestors
which leads to thunderous war woops
with each strike from either side
and an inkling that this mountain
faced world carries strong venom
within its bones

III.
A Cloudcroft cabin
made silent but snores—
spur mountain side hearth
amongst Douglas fir
Ponderosa pine

Oxygen in blood
plunged low with ascent,
phobia of heights
now validated
by the sickness of
higher altitude

Squat of breath & mirth
extravagant sleep
seems far with the strange
scent of chemicals
seeping from linens

Take the book from
olive green duffle

Gawking through thin glass
a massive black bear
drinks from a web
covered steel dog dish
left to rust on the porch

IV.
Climb faster along the hiking trail
surrounded with dense crunchy brush
silent after you asked the origin story
of my crooked nose and upper lip scar
as if distance saves from harsh truths

We all wear scars from our spirals—
cycles we set in motion,
inertia too fierce, too exhaustive
to combat long

Spider people exist—sense our
predictable movements, begin
spinning us into intricate
effective coocoons,
mummified & stunned

Only clever prey survive

V.
Damp earth
covers shoe soles,
our hands sticky
tree sap & smooth
black mud.

Breathing forest
sucks in our
passenger train,
spits us out on
the piedmont.

Conversation,
smell of earth,
& fresh cedar
lost at the
last train stop.

Indra's Net

Fibered columns of cognition form the warp
that holds our stars & wandering bodies
adrift in sporadic isolation.

With these reins the world revolves.

Fair-cheeked gods reign silent & strict with a
tongue-lagging smile from pages of mythological lore
growing jaundiced & coarse with age. The desert sand is not kind
to disappearing academic inks—youth, it seems, cannot stay gold
no matter how the yellowed gods may try. Eternal vitality
exists within the crumbled ancient text's page or damaged art
that refuses to lie any longer.

The cunning artificer plaits her silk threads
adding opulent eyes to the vast net surrounding you
& all the jewels you count look identic,
retained meticulous ad nauseam
as the cosmic spider's goldenrod threads
never fail to dance in these harsh spring sands.

The chronic incandescent baubles
preserving the sturdy spiraled double helix
from simply sweeping away with the dust &
pollen in the folds of white-hot wind.

Unbound

Female spirit,
bound to domestic
kitchen smells
white powdered soap
screams of unhappy children,
keeps her secret well.

Night conceals
lack of sleep,
man snores,
thick quilt warmth,
reality of lost dreams,
midnight blue fixed darkness.

Shutters open single window.
no cause for concern.
worries left inside
empty shell.
all that exists
is air.

With darkness comes freedom,
tight constrictive skin gone,
draped over chair
until morning—
left arm dancing
with draft.

Wind exists
for the woman
tight lipped,
shoulders tight,

bound together
by the strength
of her skin.

Snake Song

smell the earth

with a flick of tongue
creep along
stomach full of fur & teeth

scales begin to rip
& blood drains itself
on the talons of an eagle

he moves you
toward that familiar beak
pisi breath
& blank black orifice
jutting from his white feathered face

you land on the cactus
red petals blushing out of the space of struggle

pisi mi?arʉ
writhe
spit venom
curve your body back
toward musty white feathers
& strike

he forces a guttural tongue
inside your back
gurgles a reply

after sensations fade
bloody scales drop over
your deadened eyes

it's happened before
will happen again
[everyday a re-enactment
of the creation story]
& each time
you will forget

awaken in the Sonoran desert
each day to give birth
to pass egg after slimy egg
from body to dank earth
& later find part of yourself
encased in eagle's entrails

Aso & Anansi

Let your loves be like the wasp and the orchid.
　　　　　　　—Gilles Deleuze "A Thousand Plateaus"

Morning Bus

I found your pants
at the bus stop—
dusty
faded
navy blue

the left cargo pocket useless
with its large frayed hole.

We never figured out
how everything seems to happen
when you're not paying attention.

They were sprawled
over the only bench
the way you always
threw them on the couch
after coming in from work,

taking up more space
than the girls ever did.

I saw you
running down
the sidewalk

naked
except those brown thirsty boots
skin glistening with summer heat sweat—

being chased by
whatever boogieman
made you think
the pants were the problem.

Tom Robbins And The Film-Covered Penis

I was drunk & he was kind of cute,
so I took him home. When I
woke up, there was a pile of dirty
condoms on my dresser
stacked neatly in a pyramid, their
wrappers building a fence around
the base of my thrift store lamp.

I thought if I got up,
pretended to get dressed,
he'd get the hint.

He didn't move.

I told him I had a meeting to get to.
He said he'd wait for me to get back.

I didn't know what to do—so I left.
Walked around the park, smoking &
watching the boys play chess for two hours.
I came back to find the guy painting
my walls with a shit green tinted brush.

I asked if he was planning to move in.
He said not really.

Then I asked him who the fuck he thought he was.
He answered Tom Robbins.

I woke up to a purple ceiling &
gold lamé curtains. Indecipherable shapes
& words were all over my bedroom walls
in dry mud. Tom was in the kitchen,
eating raw meat from a freezer bag.

I asked him if he had a job—
something else he should be doing.
He said he writes books,
asked if I'd read them.

I told him to fuck off & went back to bed.

Woke up this time to strange smells.
He was making designs on my carpet with a
bottle of bleach. I had to get out of there.

I went to the library so I could see what the
lunatic's about. Found three books:
Skinny Legs And All,
Even Cowgirls Get The Blues,
Still Life Of A Woodpecker.
I look for pictures of the author.
That son of a bitch wasn't lying.

Couldn't read much of the books—
walking cans of pork and beans,
talking vibrators. Craziness.

I decide to go back home. I open
the door to find all my videos
smashed. Tom tore out the film
to wrap around a large paper maché
penis he built while I was gone.
He said it was the one thing
the place was missing.

I told him his books sucked ass,
the sex—awful. He gave me the finger.

I threw the penis out the window.
He ran downstairs to retrieve it.
I locked the door & started hurling
the broken plastic film cases at him
from the window. He screamed up that
he was going to leave anyway because
I was all out of Raisin Bran & good beer.

Plan B

I.
The condom broke.
The condom broke.
The condom broke.

& now we're sitting on the side
of your bed, naked in discussion.
The first serious talk we've had,
& I'm staring at the cheap plastic piece
I would tear apart with my teeth if I thought
it could feel anything like pain.

Your hair sticks up at strange angles
while you say you don't ever want kids,
say you'll pay whatever it costs to make sure,
get the pills for me even if I don't want to go.

I tell you I'll take care of it
& gather my clothes in the dark,
delete you from my phone
as I walk down the stairs,
not feeling pregnant at all.

II.
I take a long hot shower &
flush my cunt twice.
I don't feel pregnant at all, yet
I can't sleep, can't calm down &
the health center won't be open for 8 hours.
I bite my nails & look up every article
written about emergency contraception.
I read statistics, side effects, affects of kidney disease,
probability of urinary tract infections, abortion practices,
healthcare providers, reproductive rights, & legal statutes.

Now I'm pregnant.
Really truly pregnant.
I can feel your baby
moving in my uterus
& I want to scream.

I make strong coffee
& I bet you're asleep,
all snores & dreams,
as I read about RU-486, Plan B, Ella, Orval, Preven, IUDs,
estrogen, levonorgestrel, Vitamin C, massage techniques,
the days of bloody knives & folding tables, strategic stair
falls, poisonous tinctures, back alley doors, long hatpins,
knitting needles, & wire hangers.

My mind goes to dark places
as the sun finally starts to show.

III.
I sit in my car
at the grocery store
with the pharmacy
earliest to open
that carries the pills
I've decided I need.
The coffee has left me
jittery & tasting bitter
grounds on my tongue.
& the doors are opening
& I am rushing forward,
black jacket buttoned
against the wind.

Two pharmacists sit behind the glass
moving prescriptions from right to left,
gathering bottles & labels & laughing
while I wait. Their phone starts to ring;
people line up behind me. I grow warm
waiting for the window to slide from
left to right, waiting to spend money
I need for food next week to buy two
tiny overpriced pills, waiting...

She smiles & slides the glass open,
motions me to approach the counter.
My request brings audible disapproval
from the Catholic grandmother directly
behind me in line. When I turn around,
not amused, she grabs the gold cross
around her neck & whispers "Dios mio."
I give her the finger & turn back to the
window, waiting.

IV.
I am sore all over,
my body rejecting
the story of your sperm
meeting my egg
with wave upon wave
of nauseating hormones.
My skin feels electric &
all clothes, all touch end
in pain. I cry & laugh at
the same time, my emotions
unable to fit on any chart. It
hurts to lay down, it hurts to
sit. I have no energy to stand
& crawl to the bathroom when
I must. I stay in one spot for as
long as I can, reading, watching,
staring straight ahead. I cannot
imagine what pain an abortion
attempt with a hatpin would have
brought, I don't want to at all.
These damn pills are hard enough.

I cannot sleep. I cannot eat.
I drink a full gallon of water
& curse myself, curse you,
with each sip. I want to clean
everything, to shower all day
tomorrow, to drown my room
in water & soap bubbles. I want
to float on a sea of foam & warm
water until there is nothing left
of what I once was, until last night
is erased, complete. I want to wash
away to an island where no one
will ask about you ever again
& where mi coño never needs
a plan b.

The Edge Of Senlis

She buys a white dress
tailored of taffeta & silk
with what remains of her money
& packs her precious silver
deep within the folds of
fine linen cloth.

She prays to the Virgin
throughout the night,
no longer able to
rub vibrant paints on her
empty canvas without sharp pains
or mix the herbs hidden within the
base of her large wicker basket
into bottles of pungent red wine.

When dawn breaks
& she sees the sun,
she tries to think
of the lyrics she once
sang to greet the day
but it seems the words
were packed away
in the linen as well.

She washes her wrinkled skin & gathers
the thin delicate layers of white
to thrust over her imperfect
swollen body. She ties the sash
in a tight bow & puts fresh
lavender flowers in her waxy grey hair.

She walks barefoot through her marsh,
at the edge of Senlis
large basket swinging from left arm,
to harvest buds, leaves, & vines. She
wanted to feel the cool mud between
her crooked tired toes one last time &
listen to the river whisper her fortune
to its flora before she goes.

After dinner, her neighbor's daughter
stops by to deliver fish soup & discovers
the almost empty room. Piled against the
wooden table are countless painted works with
vivid scenes of river creatures & floral motifs
on hand stretched canvas.
The linen-packed silver
sits at the center with
a note addressed to her
with what paint was left
in the rusted mixing pot:

Sleep mouth open with the windows
wide & ocean spirits will whirl in.
You'll dream salty words that swim
slow around your tongue &
linger, beached, in carbonized air.

Vignettes

I.
A golden headed
four year old daughter
wet and cold
in her faded
red apron dress
hands full of dirty shirts
wades out to her mother
scrubbing clothes against
the large smooth rocks

she smiles and splashes
squishing the cake of soap
she was handed
between chubby palms and
subsequently watching
the white slippery square
follow the current
downstream

her mother
slaps her hands
and screams
to her older
bathing brothers
to catch it quick—
that cake was meant
to last one month more

II.
Ulla finds a blue dress
tailored of taffeta & silk

She washes her wrinkled skin
gathers the thin delicate layers

of bilberry & white
to thrust over her imperfect

swollen body. She has me
tie the sash in a tight bow

at the small of her back
while she puts fresh

wild lavender flowers
in her waxy grey hair.

III.
Blood stains ruined my only dress—
heather gray rayon with new random
rust blossoms across the bodice

Your apologies languish with my glare.
I toss it in the trash bin.
Disgusted.
Livid.

You salvage it,
place it flat on your table.
Then spray it, alternating
black and gold paint, until
the fabric transforms to asymmetric splendor.

I watch your sienna-skinned arms move,
mesmerized, bring warm verbena mint tea,
brush my thumb across your wet lips while
you smile & stare, transfixed by your work.

Technosexual

Good sex is like a good bridge. If you don't have a good partner, you'd better have a good hand.
— Mae West

No doubt the ancients used some primitive forms in most cases done by hand rubbing the crotch of jeans & identifying enough head to force the scow downstream a slight moan released as measured by vacuum and pressure sensors bite me on the neck suck my lower lip finger the hair before it returns to the bottom to once more engage the material straight down to her legs thighs spreading under the wooden lacquered counter that can be opened manually to allow extra water into the slurry or automatically if the suction or discharge lines begin to plug cold fingers shooting into tight panties her eyes growing wide in surprise mouth sucking air in quickly suction relief valves mounted as close to the suction mouth of the suction line as is practical with the bartender choosing this exact moment to take our empty glasses

we are all machines pistons plunging the foremost contributor panting to friction between pipe walls being velocity faster baby faster since coarse sand requires higher velocity as bright maroon lips move against thighs torso belly with an object caught in the discharge elbow drive it in hard one will feel vibration slice my back with those black painted fingernails pull the pierced nipple while closing the discharge pipe to facilitate priming of the pump tie with nylon chords add steel handcuffs when the maximum published head capacity for a pump is reached lasting about as long as the flavor in a nickel priced piece of gum re-align the parts & start again

the dipper and the grapple dredges your cock makes a scar on the center of my thoughts similar to the steam shovel snapping g strings with its teeth controlled and leather clad the result of a thorough knowledge of both the various excavating and transporting machines at its disposal her tanned moisturized legs longer than twenty minutes between thick fleshed tense thighs the greatest attention should be given to selection of machines a body radiates from the clit frontal lobe to phalanges when lips walk on my closed eyelids nipples ears neck labia brushing against my opened mouth the only difference being that the capacity is large used in surface work my lips rough and cracked at the bottom dumped into scrows run my callused fingers to her various operations use my serpent tongue like it was made with lace and satin in the shape of the clamshell or of the orange peel more she says mounted on flats I drink her big ice blue eyes move into various soils some black hair quick down through the best suited skin cheek pressed against her glossy engineer said contractor would wait watch breast to stomach as she grabs brass railing such a selection find the most efficient boot heel fetish and all she could be more economical daring stronger and laugh as if various capacity excavating had said with a razor rake my fingernails

Insight

On my secondhand couch, your head finds my lap
before I can complain or refuse.
My hand moves to curve of your skull,
short fingers drowning in smooth black hair.

I have never learned how to tell you no, with
your bristled cheek scrubbing against the fat of my thigh.
My sausage fingers drowning in your greasy black hair.
Our rough hands clasped, with harmonized pink scars.

With your cheek pressed gently against the fat of my thigh,
you make it effortless to envision our prospects.
Hands clasped tightly in harmonized flaws,
a bottle of whiskey, imported cigar.

Naturally I envision our prospects—
academic jobs, tall stacks of leather bound books,
full bottles of Gentleman Jack, Cohibas & Dominicans,
nothing but years of quiet nights of sleep or work.

Two paychecks, an entire room just for books,
two bedrooms, one bath, a place of our own
with calm nights of sleep & work.
Your muffled voice brings me back to the couch

Two bedrooms, one bath,
separate beds
I can feel the texture of the couch & strain to focus.
       I hear your voice
& my eyes are suddenly open.

Separate beds,
cleaning for two.
My eyes open wide—
no sound sleeping, no sex.

Cleaning our place after work,
always second in line for the bathroom, for food,
neither of us asleep but you still won't have sex with me—
too busy playing guitar riffs & computer games until five

Second in line,
if your friends aren't there,
playing guitar riffs & inane drinking games until five
always talking loudly of recent road trips & new tattoos.

When your friends aren't there
you'll put your arms around my neck again,
talk of driving South to get new tattoos soon.
I'll wash the dishes & nod in silent assent.

You sit up, stretch, smile, & put your arms around my neck,
my slow hands move along the hairline of your skull.
"Tell me you love me." I bite my lip. Nod in assent.
Your smile lands heavily back on my lap.

Remnants

the spider web's song,
dainty & replete is soured
after the northwest wind
spanks the passion lily's stamen

& the storm cellar's only picture book
straightens out the wonderfully odd
young stranger who'd found
the shoe-button widow's
strangled sweetheart
tangled in an incomplete silk wrapper
just outside the wooden door

today's tea must tell another's fortune
while the sugar stays thick
squatting like a swamp
amidst the thin enameled
cavity rotten teeth
of my girlfriend's mouth

the wisp of star anise & corn silk are
left alone in the wide amaretto tea pot
to stew along with the ginger tea dredges
as she holds her jaw with callused left hand,
refusing medicants with a wave of the right

& after the shortened partings,
brief hand holdings or impassioned embraces,
I wave toward the driveway
of rusted trucks moving in reverse
& sweep my caffeinated tongue
across my lips—a theater of thirst

Thirty-Five

This day each year
I wear a coffin round my neck.
Literal tarnished metal purchased
by you for me at some roadside shop
during your South Padre honeymoon.

I stare at white walls, then at opened books.
Knees pulled to stomach, left ear pressed to
my shoulder bone, rocking softly left to right
to left while people argue how to make me better.
I leave their noise to sit on the sidewalk to smoke
some USA Golds—the generic brand you always bought.

Tonight I'll dream of a February from years past.
The last family barbecue. The smell of pa's coleslaw, a cheap
yellow mix cake with chocolate frost, & you—
shoulder length ragged black hair with a grimy plastic skeleton
dangling from your right ear. Awaken once again as I hear your
manic giggle, urgent; louder than the rooster's crow.

No Sad Songs In The House Of The Sun

I.
A father taught his five-year-old
to memorize where they were
in relation to the air force base
no matter where they went:
the grocery store
church
school
her cousins' house

He said it was important
in case anything bad happens:
bombs
explosions
coordinated air attacks
& when it happened,
whatever it was,
she had to run toward the base
as fast as she could,
tearing the clothes
off her body
if she saw a sky full of smoke.

He said this would be a better,
hopefully instant death
rather than the excruciating
slow death which would happen
if she were too far away

II.
The daughter found pictures of explosions
bombs & air attacks
the next time they went to the library.

The books were thick,
so heavy the father had to help get them
from shelf to the table for her.
Books so old, so dusty,
housing lots of dark type
on bible-thin paper
with gray & black pictures
just like the old encyclopedias
her uncle had at home.

The destruction pictures
she found were funny—
like huge clouds
landed on the ground,
too tired & fat to float.

III.
A kindergarten teacher
had her class draw their family
for show & tell one day.
So the daughter drew herself, her sister,
& her dead brother
stick arms joined,
rushing toward the spot
their longer legged parents
had just abandoned on the page.
All moving closer
to the crayoned iridescent gold,
burnt orange, & dandelion waves
coming from where the air base had once been—
waxy bright waves of doom
she thought gorgeous,
like sunset hitting clean river water.

Doppelgänger

My nocturnal self has left—
lost her somewhere in Oakland
to the blacktop covered roads.

She feared the desert heat
after the coldness of the city.
Feared it'd melt her resolution,
drown out her loudest screech—
replace the hard, coal pressed hate
that serves as her grounding center
with a dripping puddle of snot.

While I wander the white & painted sand,
she frolics through asphalt & smog,
roams among drag queens & junkies
that ride the waves of Puget Sound—
making love to dreadlocked poet beggars
stealing rides on cable cars &

slicing the leash off every dog she sees
with her dad's rusty pocketknife.

Scott saw her late last week, flagged her down
from the alternate subway platform,
screaming & jumping
like someone slain in the spirit
but the only response he received was a dramatic
turn, her long braided dreads brushing the subway
floor, as she bent in full curtsey &

then a slow-blown kiss
as she walked away.

Filament, Filament, Filament

The real voyage of discovery consists not in seeking new landscapes, but in having new eyes.

—Marcel Proust, *Remembrance Of Things Past*

Animus/Anima

the delicate silver

of spider's silk:

liquid proteins

pushed through

spinnerets for:

residence

voyage

suspension

defense

capture

consumption

all from simple

gossamer thread

created by hundreds of

complementing glands

singular thread strands

set adrift or

woven in intricate patterns

utility the function—

the way Matisse

compared a painting

to an armchair—

to create

frantic &

ferocious webs

minimal &

streamline structures:

the arachnid

verve of

 art &

  acrobatics

Women Who'd Float Away

you know the type—
the ones who
a stiff wind
would turn
into parachutes,
their skinny arms
& legs flailing
like abandoned
kite strings
during an upscale
wind event,
armpits larger than
the cartoonish ocular
cavity painted with the
red vocal punching
bag at back but
always shaven close
to the sensitive burred
skin that holds aversion
to the contents of aerosol cans or
masculine scents

When Clouds Sizzle

The surrounding sky goes aflame—
becomes a billion flecks of bright
amber & crimson glowing embers
that float on Eurus' wretched burned back.
The lizard brain's attempt of flight
& panic is stowed as a chorus
of childish laughter sweeps
across the yellowed grass.

A sea of tiny shadowed palms reach high
beyond their hooded heads, grasping towards
the beautiful warm flickering specks swirling
above as bundled grownups breathe deeply into the
disposable coffee cups held close to their hearts.

There are thoughts that only occur when clouds sizzle—
their moist fluff dissolved to a faint smell of wet smoke.
Suspended & muddy thoughts losing composition
like the ash of a thirty foot effigy burnt with a city's
worth of worry. Important thoughts that dissipate
when the air is no longer heavy of soot & blaze,
your neck now sore from the chin's vigilant
upward thrust while lungs begin to recover
from their once reliable humid hearth.

Song for Nina
for N.S.

There are no palm trees
in the streets—

only dirt
and busted glass
to show my reflection

and while Tulsa isn't
Chicago
same damn thing—

concrete buildings,
folks who'd rather
spit on ya than talk

to ya.

Goddamn it Nina
tell me I'm beautiful
tell me I'm real

real as rivers,
real as warm biscuits
in the morning

and red beans at night.

There's no palm trees,
     no rivers
in the streets,

but you were there
right alongside me
and you knew

we all knew
your deep
dry voice

sings the refrain

moves our arms
to flail,
to beat like wings

unbroken.
Mend us
with words
and melodies sung
in our voice
    our tongue

you don't have
to speak Nina.
Just take me

to the water,

take me home.

we have lived like this
we want the little country
farm,

our hands cracked

calloused

backs strong
like your voice
    your song.

Take me home Nina
back where I

    where you

    where we

    was born.

Take me home,
love me
cause your love is
the wind
through palm trees.

Xing

We need to walk to know sacred places, those around us & those within. We need to walk to remember the songs.
—Joseph Bruchac

Maps are not made for pedestrians—
the easy to follow pale white & yellow grids
all equally measured in sound neat little squares
do not guide our calloused feet to their stated destinations.

Like the 4 homeless men & the frayed lavender handbag
haunting the park benches in Franklin Square, we are
stuck in an existing realistic point manifested on an imaginary
political line that decides past this specific blade of grass &
before that spewing busted bottle we have crossed onto new
territory, different from that before it & so named
in a digital nomenclature of Arabic origins.

Yes, we can feel the difference from 7th to 6th—
textures more sharp & ragged as the digits decrease,
but is this texture something inherit to the digits themselves
or is it indicative of this spot of land? More directly: where
did the infection start—within the word or the identifiable
core chemical bonds? Does this sharpness stem from the steady
linear mark, creating a perpendicular intersection? Or has it
always been there, eroding any smooth clavicle corners into
thorn shaped cement knives waiting to puncture supple skin?

None of us get closer to where we want to be here, the
feeling of yesterday's rainstorm gropes our toes/ankles/calves
until the puddles have grown to the size of the Delaware & no one
is left in our battalion to forge the way ahead. We are forced then
to become river walking saints to continue on our path, or
walk shamefaced back along the cobblestone streets & cement
bypasses we scorched earlier to arrive at this water's den.

Respite

I.
We have time before
the Greyhound stops
the drugs kick in
a drop or two left in our glasses
& the not so small hope to
see something good

Bewitched by an endless rancid
& phallic argument
while saddled between two friends
in a fast moving car on its way
to the unwholesome theater aisle
where we've been bastardized
season after season,
my cigarette is left to die on the
constantly sticky floor

Inside we toast one another
from smuggled metal flasks
& pocket bottles of Jack Daniels
seek the acidic sweet taste of lemon fruit snacks
unwrapped from individual stolid cellophane
& mix these tastes with the artificial butter flavor
from someone's abandoned popcorn
as our stomachs grumble a chorus of approval

This is life's reverie
dubbed as reference:
to grandeur, to prisons,
to monotonous mentions
of Quentin Tarantino tropes
Raymond Chandler genius
& Toni Collette's teeth

II.
What is left of brightness
when its shine shimmers
against dusty black backdrops
 & maroon carpet covered walls
in the low rent surround sound caves
we frequent—plugged into mp3 noise
control or talking in whispers—
deaf to the dwindling Dachau belle
left alone, stilted, upstaged
by a scratched sandalwood sofa
& cracked cherry wood chaise lounge?

What does this product rich culture have to offer us
outside of the momentary relief of a stadium seated
air-conditioned womb? We, the mayo covered masses
who print our names on each job application so that
we'll be able to wipe the table once you leave,
bring you house salad w/ the dressing on the side,
return your unwanted salmon filet & sing your
daughter or friend happy birthday?

Where can we go to swim in the tranquil sea
day spa of your experience? Surely, it isn't
to be found amongst the unmoving
cup holders, the blue glow of aisle lights,
& overflowing metal cans of trash we pass

III.
We exist in the haze of sleeplessness
& intoxication, where the whole vast world
feels fuzzy & off balance,
the passage of time measured in weary bones,
wrinkled skin, old band shirts, faded hair colors,
& uncounted collections of stolen shot glasses

We are the ones that leave raucous & early
to avoid long lines for bathroom stalls,
tear horror movie posters from their wall carpet home
to fold haphazard & smuggle out in back pockets,
snort expensive white powder at the mirror,
or dry swallow multi-colored caps
in full view of ricochet children without mothers
& smoking employees hiding from their mops

We are the ones who throw abandoned cups at
large pristine mirrors & find seats in
adjacent high priced nightmares
without tickets, laughing loudly, & put our
feet up on the back of your seat,
the demand for free air conditioning
too high in this relentless desert heat

The Judd Nelson Habit

Cheese-covered teeth document
the in-group's toothy grins
but open this up & out beyond
swapping bruises to chilled champagne,
snorting lines & cheap paté, take it
from Muscle Beach to the Louver,
refusing to drive through Torrance
or Englewood, & Amsterdam's
only for beginners. What else can we
use to break the Judd Nelson habit?
Wearing the suit's not enough.
You must own it, charge it, & with
our career it's not considered
a job related expense. Make it
around the next five traumas—no breaks,
no signal, just a dusty path
in your wake.

Wing

Someone left an intact left wing on the sidewalk.
There are no signs of foul play—
no feathers floating in the blades of grass nearby
or remnants of a mangled body in the bike lane.
There is only this wing, intact, perfect, as if the bird
dropped it. Like a prosthetic the bird forgot to knot in place.

Brown & dusty, spread as if for one last dive
into uncharted air space over the sweltering lot
of gleaming metal & fiberglass automobiles,
the feathers seeking one last taste of air borne escape.

I want to pick up the wing, claim it for my own.
Grow it longer overnight in a Petri dish the size of an
inflatable kiddie pool & then strap it onto my arm
& run around like a modern day Icarus.

I want to shrink the thing, place it inside a clear plastic case
& carry this wing with me inside my black faded messenger bag.
I want to take it with me for show & tell for each of my classes—
to prove to my students that it is possible to
reach the stars with a little help from Gaia, that we can all
grow expandable brown feathered wings out of our shoulder sockets &
reach beyond the fruit on the tallest branches. That with enough wind & sky
you can make the impossible the obtainable & leave this infamous land of
entrapment for the enormous sand bound cockroaches.

I stand there long enough to see this backfire, my hardened talented students
who have had their arms & legs broken in their youth by older stronger animals
shaking their heads as I cup the delicate feathers of the wing in my palms & begin
my speech. My beautiful war scarred students limping to & from class with
metal shrapnel still embedded in their knees staring directly into my optimistic
heart with the blank darkness of their eyes as I offer up the shreds of my hope for
them, for their futures away from this dank cave of a classroom. I see them
snicker one to another, meeting their friends & partner's faces with similar snark
& mirth—making jokes en Español or Diné under their breath
when they are convinced I cannot hear or understand them.

77

I stand above the wing, looking down at it, afraid to move, to touch it. Afraid that if I do, the bird will come back, angry that I tried to steal something so blatantly not mine. Afraid the bird spirits will hunt me for trying too hard to become something I am not meant to be. Afraid that the moment I touch it, the perfection—the intact-ness, the glory of this dusty wing will dissipate into the desert sand & I will be alone, late for class with nothing but a broken feather in my hand. I wish that I could delicately pick the wing up & run without any traffic mishaps or light delays, & take it straight home. Spend the day studying it–aerodynamics & wingspan, measuring the primary & secondary feathers, tracing the curve of the wing with my fingers, gauging weight, lift, drag, & thrust. I want to do nothing else but be with this wing

But I do not. I sigh heavily & move out of the walking path of the groups of students hurrying past. I speak silently to the bird spirits above in care of their people. I wish the wing well onto its next home & hurry forth into the dust bringing spring winds, onward to the incredibly important work of instructors.

On Guadalupe Bridge

Seven thin concrete slabs with the Virgen's visage, nuestra querida, guard the east exit & I need no rearview mirror to tell me Los Virgens have turned their back to us.

Joe, the homeless vet that rides my bus sometimes, balls up his dirt crusted fist & pounds on the hood of my Olds as he crosses between idling cars. White smoke blooms from the cracks between body & the hood. "Your car's too goddamned loud," he shouts towards my cracked windshield, then spits on the concrete near my front tire. I nod & yell back "What'd you say? Can't hear you over the engine."

He pushes his face close to the slit in my front window & says "I ASKED FOR A GODDAMNED CIGARETTE. YOUR CAR'S MAKING MY LUNGS JEALOUS." I laugh & show him the empty pack riding shotgun. He snarls & shakes his head, starts knocking on the car next to mine.

"Oooooo Mami, que pasa?" "Está caliente. Caliente Caliente...es verdad." I wave away the group of greasy construction workers with one hand & fan my face with a magazine with the other. The heat is intense & I've stripped every layer of clothes I can without getting arrested. The car has no air conditioner, the side windows' glass has broken off the busted tracks so they refuse to roll up or down on command. It shouldn't be legal to keep us in traffic so long during desert summers. Kendric's told me people die this way. Marco, the paletas pushcart guy weaves his way along the median, selling cold sweets, water, & large bags of chicharrones to the victims of the evening commute, our tires stuck like they've melted permanent to the pavement, only those on foot getting ahead on Guadalupe Bridge.

My jaw's locked & I grind my teeth, drum my thumbs against the sticky driving wheel. Once again I wish my stereo was still mine even though I maxed the speakers out trying to hear music over the loud clacking of the engine. Today Carlos is sitting nearby in his low riding Lincoln, playing Tejano to drown out his boys fighting in the back. I can barely hear more than the loud bursts of bass but I watch teenage fists fly back and forth as Carlos shakes his head, rolls up the window, speaks & motions with his own fist in the rearview mirror. Everyone stuck in Tejano hell or maybe just this particular traffic purgatory, their hearts tired of pounding, tongues swollen all thirsty & hot, spending the rest of eternity on the overpass of Guadalupe Bridge.

Guionista Sangre (Blood Writer)

carved into her flesh
    face & breast
        ink maps the path of blood
        from the lip pivot to nipple
        down the broken line
           like water
             dripping rusted letters
             to the faucet's mouth
                guionista sangre
        expression by cuts from the lips
                      ears
                      tongue
                      chin
                          bloodied vulva—
                          bloodied foreheads
                    embellished scars

                    *

they rub the letters
        letters of dirt
        letters of stars
        letters of blood on
                a woman of the water:
                the moon bleeder
                      branded
                      tattooed from the area
                      around eyes
                      down to breasts
                          covered with paths:
                          cultural maps

guionista sangre
in stone & memory
in breasts & feathers
    they are hungry
        hungry for daylight
  alien roads
  potent tongues

su sangre holds its own power
    its own map
      its own love letters written in cement ponds
      & su coño embodies it

        *

we've never been taught geography
  never known the contours of ourselves
    one's own body is a cavern filled with
    bandages & wounds
      & medicine functions as a defective breastplate
        or an elaborate plot to bind Kali's treacherous feet
        before letters fly from Babylon's highest towers
        & the broken red clay children refuse to kneel
            bow their sun baked heads
            raise their calloused
            bloodstained hands
                to the dark clouds
                & wait

        *

her vulva makes the sky form
　　　　　　the holy v
　　　　　　　　　she rises from the sea
　　　　　　　　　foam born blood & man
　　　　　　　　　　　　　　　would nail her to the littoral
　　　　　　　　　　　　　　　　　make her literal
　　　　　　　　recycle su sangre for
　　　　　　　　Cover girl lip shade palates
　　　　　　　　　　　　no end spread round a woman
　　　　　　　　　　　　no end

　　　　　　　　　　　*

　　　　　　　she rises from the rock
　　　　　　　a breast-fat lady holding high a drink horn
　　　　　　　with a broken handle
　　　　　　　　　　las curanderas chant in unison
　　　　　　　　　　& cryptic letters appear
　　　　　　　　　　in supple fluid lines & the orishas begin to
　　　　　　　　　　twirl & spit twisted black letters:
　　　　　　　　　　　　exploded pods
　　　　　　　　　　　　　　that split cow & calf & sow in
　　　　　　　　　　　　　　silent wetness
　　　　　　　　　　　　　　　　split elastic water that
　　　　　　　　　　　　　　　　flows & shouts to
　　　　　　　　　　　　mothers of openings
　　　　　　　　　　　　　　　mothers of change in
　　　　　　　　　　　　　　bubbled water that sees them
　　　　　　　　　spinning spitting speaking in
　　　　　　　　　　　　　　　　　　lenguas rotas
　　　　　　　　　　　　　　　　　　signos rotas

　　　　　　　　　　　*

blackened fingers stroking painted lips
with bowed little faces at their breast that growl & bite & hiss
that wait for moon water & stories
    wait para su sangre para llegar
        from between smooth unmarked thighs
        from their chins & lips:
            blood to make strength visible
            in careful black scarred letters

                & the women smile at the breastfed young
                wrapping small fingers around their loose
                            coiled hair
            while water drifts
            from their muddied feet

                *

& you
you think about us
    about the vulva

        because other women
        bleed for babies

            but we—
            la guionista sangre--
            we bleed for stories

                (*hijos ingratos*)
                children
                that can never
                be made whole

A Full Measure's Rest

As I opened my mouth to speak

no words

no sound

escaped

which left me full astonished

that I might have unlearned

the world of phonetics

unwound the belts & chains

on my tongue

refusing to find new ones

or re-fuel

the motorized cement mortar

previously caked

in the interior walls

of a dusty throat

the unconscious

yet calculated refusal

driving my tonsils

to dance

my esophagus

to sing

& self assured vocal chords

to slouch

rotate their tired necks

& begin massaging

knotted muscles

Glossary of Potentially Unfamiliar Terms

taabe—sun
corrido—Mexican folk ballad
cerca de tu cuerpo—circle around your body
marɨawe—Nɨmɨnɨɨ greeting meaning "tell me your story"
todas las noches para una semana—every night for a week
en el trailer amarillo—in the yellow trailer
para el baño—for the bathroom
comer pasta de dientes en una tostada—to eat toothpaste on toast
veinticinco—25
y en mi cama—and in my bed
en nuestro apartamento—in our apartment
nuestra madre—our mother
alta de la meth—high on meth
hacernos tostadas—make us toast
aikɨrekwatɨ—talk wrong
kwana kuhtsu paa—the Rio Grande
u?hoiki mɨhɨ naape—around your feet
sitzkrieg—slow moving warfare marked by repeated stalemate
mɨa—moon
yutaibo—Mexican
pisi—rotten infested festered
pisi mi?arɨ—becoming infected
mi coño—my pussy
nuestra querida—our dear
paletas—popsicles
chicharrones—pork rinds
Tejano—direct translation is Texan, but is also the name of folk and popular music originating from Mexican American populations of Texas.
las curanderas—traditional healers
orishas—Yoroba spirit/manifestation of diety
lenguas rotas—broken tongues
signos rotas—broken signs
hijos ingratos—ungrateful children

NOTES

~Antes Taabe (Before the Sun)
This poem's content was inspired by research about Aztec gods and goddesses, particularly the origin story of Huitzilopochtli (god of sun and war). It codeswitches between English, Nʉmʉ Tekwapʉha (Comanche), and Spanish languages.

Spin Cycle
Song lyrics included in this poem come from (in order of appearance) The Carter Family's "I'm Thinking Tonight of My Blue Eyes," James Whitcomb Riley's "Shortnin' Bread," Darrell Scott's "Long Time Gone," & Carl Newman's "The Laws Have Changed."

From Wind & Earth
The creation of this poem was inspired by the Nʉmʉnʉʉ creation story, where the Nʉmʉnʉʉ people were created by the Great Spirit from dust swirls from each of the four directions.

One Clover, One Bee
This poem is a response to Emily Dickinson's poem "To Make a Prairie (1755)."

Indra's Net
The content of this poem is inspired by Buddhist teachings. Indra's Net is a metaphor used to illustrate the concepts of Śūnyatā (emptiness), pratītyasamutpāda (dependent origination), and interpenetration in Buddhist philosophy. It refers to the net that hangs over the Vedic god Indra's palace. Indra's net has a multifaceted jewel at each vertex, and each jewel is reflected in all of the other jewels. In the Avatamsaka Sutra, this image is used to describe the interconnectedness of the universe.

Unbound
This poem was inspired by a West Indies folktale within the book *Black Ice* by Lorene Cary. In the tale, a woman leaves her husband asleep in their bed each night before taking her skin off and flying

away. She is careful to return before he wakes, but one night he wakes to find her gone. He sees the empty skin. Upset by her leaving, he rubs salt inside the skin. When she returns, she cannot wear her skin any longer.

Snake Song
This poem's content invokes the imagery of the Mexican flag—an eagle with a serpent in its beak perched on a cactus.

Technosexual
This poem was created through mixing the descriptions of the working parts of old dredging boats and machines with sexual acts. The dredge terms were researched within *Dredges And Dredging* by Charles Prelini.

When Clouds Sizzle
This poem was written on the occasion of the 2012 burning of "El Kookooee," a 30 year old Albuquerque South Valley tradition. "El Kookooee," or "El Koko," is a thirty foot tall wooden monster that represents fear. Local residence write down their personal fears on pieces of paper that are then collected and burned with the monster. The annual burning is meant as a catharsis that strengthens the community individually and as a whole.

Song for Nina
This poem was written on the occurrence of Nina Simone's death on April 21, 2003. The poem "No Image" by William Waring Cuny was used as inspiration as it was performed by Simone as a song she called "Images."

Guionista Sangre (Blood Writer)
This poem codeswitches between English and Spanish. The contents were inspired from research into the historical and cultural practices based around menstruation. The book *Blood, Bread, and Roses: How Menstruation Created the World* by Judy Grahn was exceedingly helpful.

Shauna Osborn is an award-winning Nʉmʉnʉʉ (Comanche) / German mestiza artist, musician, researcher, secret agent, and wordsmith. She has a BA from the University of Oklahoma and an MFA from New Mexico State University. In 2013, she received a National Poetry Award from the New York Public Library, which left her indebted to their social media coordinator for placing one of her poems between a photo of David Tennant reading a library book and an announcement for a William Gibson reading. She was a 2015 Artist in Residence at A Room of Her Own Foundation's Writing Retreat, where she began her photography project called Carved Skin. Shauna has also received the Luminaire Award from Alternating Current Press and the Native Writer Award from UNM Summer Writers' Conference. *Arachnid Verve* is her debut poetry collection.